LB-ACW 003

Civil War Sketch Book 3 Illustrations by Edwin Austin Forbes

Luca Stefano Cristini
color plates by Edwin Austin Forbes 1839-1895

SOLDIERSHOP PUBLISHING

AUTHORS

Edwin Austin Forbes (1839 – March 6, 1895) was a famous American landscape painter and etcher who first gained fame during the American Civil War for his detailed and dramatic sketches of military subjects, including battlefield combat scenes. Forbes was born in New York, studied under Arthur Fitzwilliam Tait. During the Civil War, he was special artist for Frank Leslie's Magazine. Many of the spirited etchings he drew during the conflict were later presented by General Sherman to the government. They are now preserved in the War Office at Washington because of their historic value.
He died in 1895 in Brooklyn and is interred in Green-Wood Cemetery.

Luca Stefano Cristini has edited various publications on ancient and contemporary historical themes, including books on thirty years war, Medieval, Napoleonic as well as several illustrated books with historical color photographs. He has also curated all the brands of Soldiershop publishing. Here is the author of preface, text and captions.

PUBLISHING'S NOTE

None of **unpublished** images or text of our book may be reproduced in any format without the expressed written permission of Soldiershop.com when not indicate as marked with license creative commons 3.0 or 4.0. The publisher remains to disposition of the possible having right for all the doubtful sources images or not identifies. Our trademark: Soldiershop Publishing ©, The names of our series: Soldiers&Weapons, Battlefield, War in colour, PaperSoldiers, Soldiershop e-book etc. are herein © by Soldiershop.com.

NOTE ABOUT BOOK PRINTING BEFORE 1925

This book may contain text or images coming from a reproduction of a book published before 1925 (over seventy years ago). No effort has been made to modernize or standardize the spelling used in the original text, so this book may have occasional imperfections such as missing or blurred pages, poor pictures, errant marks, etc. that were either part of the original artifact, or were introduced by the scanning process. We believe this work is culturally important, and despite the imperfections, have elected to bring it back into print (digital and/or paper) as part of our continuing commitment to the preservation of printed works worldwide. We appreciate your understanding of the imperfections in the preservation process, and hope you enjoy this valuable book. Now this book is purpose re-built and is proof-read and re-type set from the original to provide an outstanding experience of reflowing text, also for an ebook reader. However Soldiershop publishing added, enriched, revised and overhauled the text, images, etc. of the cover and the book. Therefore, the job is now to all intents and purposes a derivative work, and the added, new and original parts of the book are the copyright of Soldiershop. On this second unpublished part of the book none of images or text may be reproduced in any format without the expressed written permission of Soldiershop. Almost many of the images of our books and prints are taken from original first edition prints or books that are no longer in copyright and are therefore public domain. We have been a specialized bookstore for a long time so we (and several friends antiquarian booksellers) have readily available a lot of ancient, historical and illustrated books not in copyright. Each of our prints, art designs or illustrations is either our own creation, or a fully digitally restoration by our computer artists, or non copyrighted images. All of our prints are "tagged" with a registered digital copyright. Soldiershop remains to disposition of the possible having right for all the doubtful sources images or not identifies.

LICENSES COMMONS

This book may utilize material marked with license creative commons 3.0 or 4.0 (CC BY 4.0), (CC BY-ND 4.0), (CC BY-SA 4.0) or (CC0 1.0). We give appropriate attribution credit and indicate if change were made below in the acknowledgements field.

ACKNOWLEDGEMENTS

A Special Thanks to LC (library of Congress) and other institutions for their kindly permission to use some images of his archives, collections or books used in our book.

Title: **Civil War sketch book 3 - Illustrations by Edwin Austin Forbes**
By Luca S. Cristini & Anna Cristini. Plates by E.A.Forbes. First edition by Soldiershop. June 2020
Cover & Art Design: Luca S. Cristini. ISBN code: 978-88-93276009
Published by Luca Cristini Editore, via Orio 35/4- 24050 Zanica (BG) ITALY. www.soldiershop.com

Edwin Austin Forbes 1839-1895

Pursuit of Lee's army. Scene on the road near Emmitsburg, marching through the rain, July 7 1863, by Edwin Forbes. Library of Congress

EDWIN FORBES, THE WAR ARTIST OF LESLIE'S WEEKLY

Many films have been made about the American Civil War and yet many books have been written. At the same time, the American Civil War was the first major conflict to leave behind an extensive photographic record. However, perhaps not everyone is aware of another form available to understand the feelings that those terrible years brought with them: drawings. One of the factors that make these sketches, drawn on any available material, particularly interesting is that they may be a better instrument for capturing movements, actions or emotions than the photographs of the time. In both the photographic record and the more official war art, as engaging as they can be, there does seem to be something important missing: the immediacy and intimacy of everyday life as a soldier. Unlike photographs, which shoot and immortalize a precise and unrepeatable moment, drawing is not so immediate. The artist needs time to represent what his eye is observing, and in this time the subject actually changes, he moves, he's dynamic. If one can imagine drawing a battle, it is automatic to think about the speed of the hand and the "schizophrenia" of the drawing that will result, and it is precisely this stylistic nervousness that manages to make those who have never experienced war, fortunately, understand how inglorious it can be. At the same time, we can admire drawings made in moments of calm and camaraderie between soldiers: moments of everyday life in which you can read on the faces of the characters portrayed tiredness, homesickness, scars and wounds of war… And rarely smiles. Many of the drawings that we will present later on have their respective captions written by the authors, and thanks to them we discover more details about the scene described. The authors we will consider in these volumes are three: Adolph Metzner, Edwin Forbes and William Waud.

Edwin Austin Forbes was born in New York in 1839. Very young, he studied with Arthur Fitzwilliam Tait, a British-American artist known mostly for his paintings of wildlife. From him, Forbes he inherited the passion and learnt the secrets of landscape and animal painting. Showing a great talent from the beginning, and in 1861, at the age of twenty-two he shouldered his portfolio of papers, pencils, chalks, and inks, and was hired from the *Frank Leslie's Illustrated Newspaper* (sometimes also referred to simply as *Frank Leslie's Magazine* or *Leslie's Weekly*), as a special war artist. He was assigned by Leslie to cover the Army of the Potomac in 1862, and did so until the Siege of Petersburg in 1864, also spending time with other Union armies. When the American Civil War broke out, one of the most brilliant and famous editor of New York City said: "This war will absorb public attention and be the ruin of the newspapers", not imaging how wrong he was. Of course the conflict had all eyes on it, therefore it was the *making* of the newspapers. The correspondents in the capital and in the field leaped to their opportunity, developing elements of quickness, sagacity and comprehension that were potent factors of public education in all that the war was, and among others artists, as we have seen on the other volumes of this series, Edwin Forbes's sketches were some of the most appreciated. In his daring pursuit of information, his pictures in the very midst of the varied scenes of camp, marching days, hospital, bivouac and battlefields made his reality, and the one of thousands of soldiers, familiar to the home public through the illustrated papers of the day.

Among the similitudes with the first artist we took under consideration, Adolph Metzner, there are many stylistic differences between him and Forbes. This one, as we said above, came from a natural and landscaping background, with a special attention on animals. While Metzner played with pathos, emotions and mockeries between comrades, he was more into the subjects' realistic details and definition. Another big difference between the two is that Metzner did find some sort of relief from the war he was not only drawing but fighting too, being the Captain of the 32nd Regiment Indiana Volunteer Infantry, while for Edwin Forbes it was his job: a painter, now war correspondent. Although he had marched for two years together with the Potomac Army, being on-hand to witness the battles of Cedar Mountain, Second Battle of Bull Run (Second Manassas), Antietam, Chancellorsville, Gettysburg, the Wilderness, and Petersburg he was never able to get dangerously close to the battle without endangering his life. That's why we often see how he used to sit on a distant point from where he could portray a wider scene, cities, battles or even the July 4th reconnaissance work being performed by Sykes' 5th Corps. He seems to have great confidence with perspective notions, and many of these landscapes are enriched by brisk details or notations to better locate the setting of what he was witnessing, a part of an accurate caption too. Daily camp life and incidents in the field were among his favorite subjects to draw, and yet we can see also a curious collection of equines subjects such as horses and donkeys. We can really appreciate the affection he had for his mare, Kitty, because she has been portrayed in many occasions.

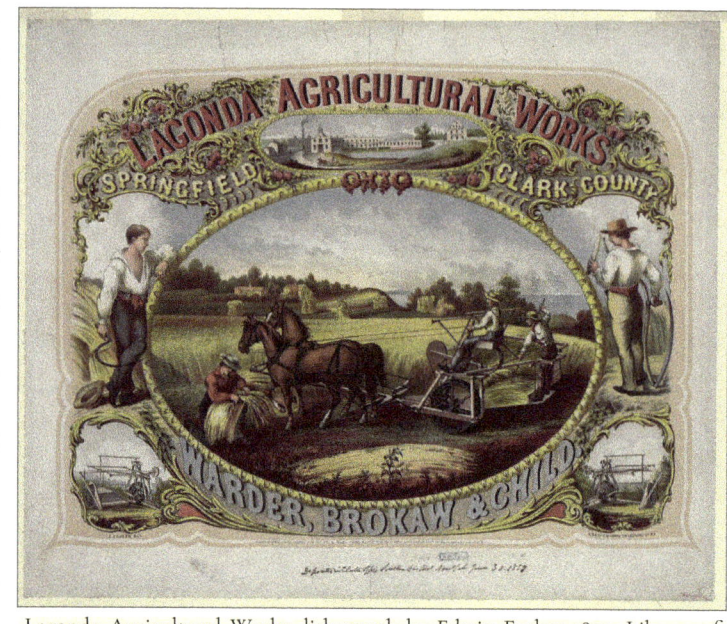

Lagonda Agricultural Works, lithograph by Edwin Forbes 1859. Library of Congress. an example of the artist's great ability also in the field of the then-born advertising graphics.

After trekking with the Army of Potomac for two years and a half, he left before the mine explosion of July 30th and returned to his native New York in the autumn of 1864. He left the newspaper without explanation and was replaced by artist Edward Mullen. Before quitting his job Forbes reclaimed his original sketches from his employer, who in the mean time had already reproduced a half of them to be converted into woodcuts for printing, and began to work on his greatest artistic achievement. In three years, from 1865 to 1868, he completed the drawings of forty scenes based on his wartime sketches attached together to create what was called "*Life Studies of the Great Army*" a few years later. After showing his etchings to General William T. Sherman, this one was so impressed that he presented Forbes' work to the government, and even purchased a set of plates for his office in the War Department in Washington. In 1876 the International Art Commission at the Centennial Exposition in Philadelphia gave Forbes the highest award in their power, a gold medal, privately expressing their wonder that one man should have been able to produce such a splendid array of artistic plates. In 1877 he was made an honorary member of the London Etching Club. Five years before his death he published a book titled *An Artist's Story of the Great War* then died in 1895 in Brooklyn and was interred in Green-Wood Cemetery.

What is perhaps of more interest to us in these present days is that Forbes' pictures are in very truth "life studies", and reproduce with startling realism the almost forgotten minutiae of the scenes they portray, the beauty and the tragedy, the brightness and the dullness, and the infinite variety of picturesque facts in all arms of the service. If in the previous volume of this series we have seen how Adolph Metzner used berries or fruits to create the colors he needed to paint, Edwin Forbes was not so experimental, he was an artist in the most classic sense of the term. Most of his sketches (a part of those he retouched after the war) are in black and white, although a beautiful color series dedicated to the Battle of Gettysburg is particularly well known. After they were acquired by the Library of Congress in 1919, it's the first time someone, in this case our digital artists, retouches Forbes' wonderful pictures adding some color to them, somehow inheriting his mission: to give even more *life* to his "*Life Studies*", making this volume an unmissable piece of art collection for every fan of the American Civil War.

THE PLATES
GETTYSBURG & 1863

Soldiers' huts in winter camp, January 12 1863

Building a chimney, January 15 1863

Sketch of officer of infantry. The colonel, February 10 1863

Study of infantry soldier on guard. William J. Jackson, Sergt. Maj. 12th N.Y. Vols. Sketched at Stoneman's Switch, near Fredricksburg, Va. Jan. 27th, 1863

Cavalry outpost, near Potomac Creek. Daybreak on a cold morning, February 10 1863

Stragglers on the march to headquarters. Under guard, February 10 1863

The gov't. steamboat Wilson Small at Acquia Creek, March 12, 1863

Picket station on Potomac Creek, March 13 1863

St. Patrick's Day in the army. A hurdle race, March 17 1863

St. Patrick's Day in the army. The grand stand, March 17 1863

On picket. Officers' quarters in log house, March 18 1863

Railroad train containing President Lincoln crossing Potomac Creek bridge on his way to review the Army of the Potomac, April 5 1863

President Lincoln reviewing the Army of the Potomac on Monday, April 6, 1863

Review of the Army of the Potomac, commanded by Gen. Joe E. Hooker, by President Abraham Lincoln, April 6 1863

A siesta The defenses of Centreville, forts, breastworks, etc.; from a point south of the Warrenton turnpike, April 18 1863, 1861

Kelly's Ford - Stonemans raid, April 21st 1863

The battle of Chancellorsville. Scene at junction of U.S. ford road, and road to Rapidan River, April 30 1863

The Army of the Potomac, on the march to Chancellorsville, April 30 1863

The battle of Chancellorsville, April 30 1863

Scene on the U.S. ford road (battle of Chancellorsville) on the night of Apr. 30, 1863

In the woods at Chancellorsville. Bivouac at night, April 30 1863

Sketches on the line of march. Bucktails, April 30 1863

Gen. Hooker's headquarters at the Chancellorsville house, May 1 1863

Field hospital (second corps) on the battlefield of Chancellorsville, May 2 1863

Rebel prisoners and battle flags captured at Chancellorsville, being taken to the rear by cavalry and infantry guards, May 3 1863

Attack on Gen. Sedwick's Corps. Banks Ford near Chancellorsville, seen from the north bank of the Rappahannock River, May 4 1863

A breakdown in the wagoner's camp, May 6 1863

Just from Chancellorsville. An amateur quartermaster, May 6 1863

Attack on the Union position at the Chancellorsville House, May 10 1863

Departure of two-years men from the Army of the Potomac. A scene near Falmouth, Va., May 20 1863

Charge of cavalry under Genl. Pleasonton supported by the 1st division of the 5th Corps near Ashby's Gap June 21 1863

Cavalry fight near Aldie, Va. During the march to Gettysburg; the Union Cavalry, commanded by Gen. Pleasonton, the Confederate by J.E.B. Stuart June 24 1863

Grand review of Gen. N.P. Banks's Corps at Little Washington, Va. June 25 1863

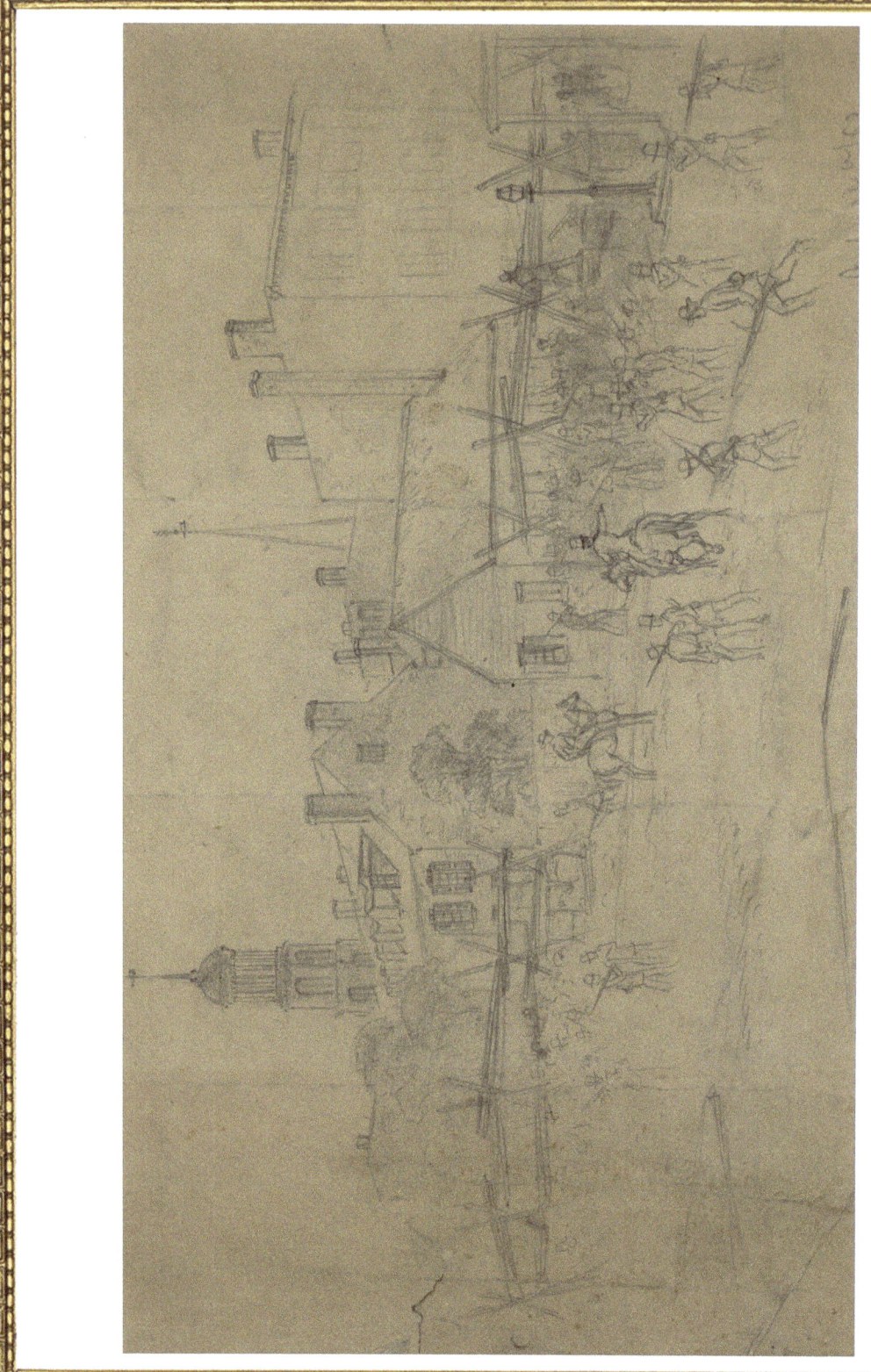

Scene in Baltimore, Md. Citizens building barricades on receipt of the news of Gen. Lee's march into Penn. June 28 1863

The battle of Gettysburg July 1 1863

The battle of Gettysburg. Attack on the Third Corps, Gen. Daniel E. Sickles, by Gen. Longstreet's Corps, July 2 1863

The battle of Gettysburg. The gateway of the cemetery, the center of the Union position, First and Eleventh Corps July 2 1863

Attack on Little Round Top held by the 5th Corps commanded by General Sykes, July 2 1863

The battle of Gettysburg. View from the summit of Little Round Top. The advance of Genl. Longstreet's Corps on the Union position (5th Corps) on Little Round Top, Thursday evening and Friday afternoon, July 2 1863

Attack of Genl Ewell's Corps (Johnston's division), on the right flank of the Union Army on Culp's Hill held by the 12th Corps (Gen. Slocum) during the battle of Gettysburg, July 2 1863

Attack of Johnston's Div., C.S.A. on the breastworks on Culp's Hill defended by Wadsworth's Div., 1st Corps, and a part of the 12th Corps [under] General Slocum, half past seven P.M. July 2 1863

General view of the Union lines on the morning of July 3rd, 10 AM, during the attack of Johnston's Div. C.S.A., 1863

The battle of Gettysburg July 3 1863

A lull in the Picketts charge on the Union centre at the grove of trees about 3 P M, July 3 1863 fight, 1861

Picketts charge from a position on the enemys line looking toward the Union lines, Zieglers grove on the left, clump of trees on right, July 3 1863

Charge of Ewell's Corps on the cemetery [i.e. cemetery] gate and capture of Ricketts Battery, July 3 1863

View from the summit of Little Round Top at 7.30 P.M. July 3rd, 1863

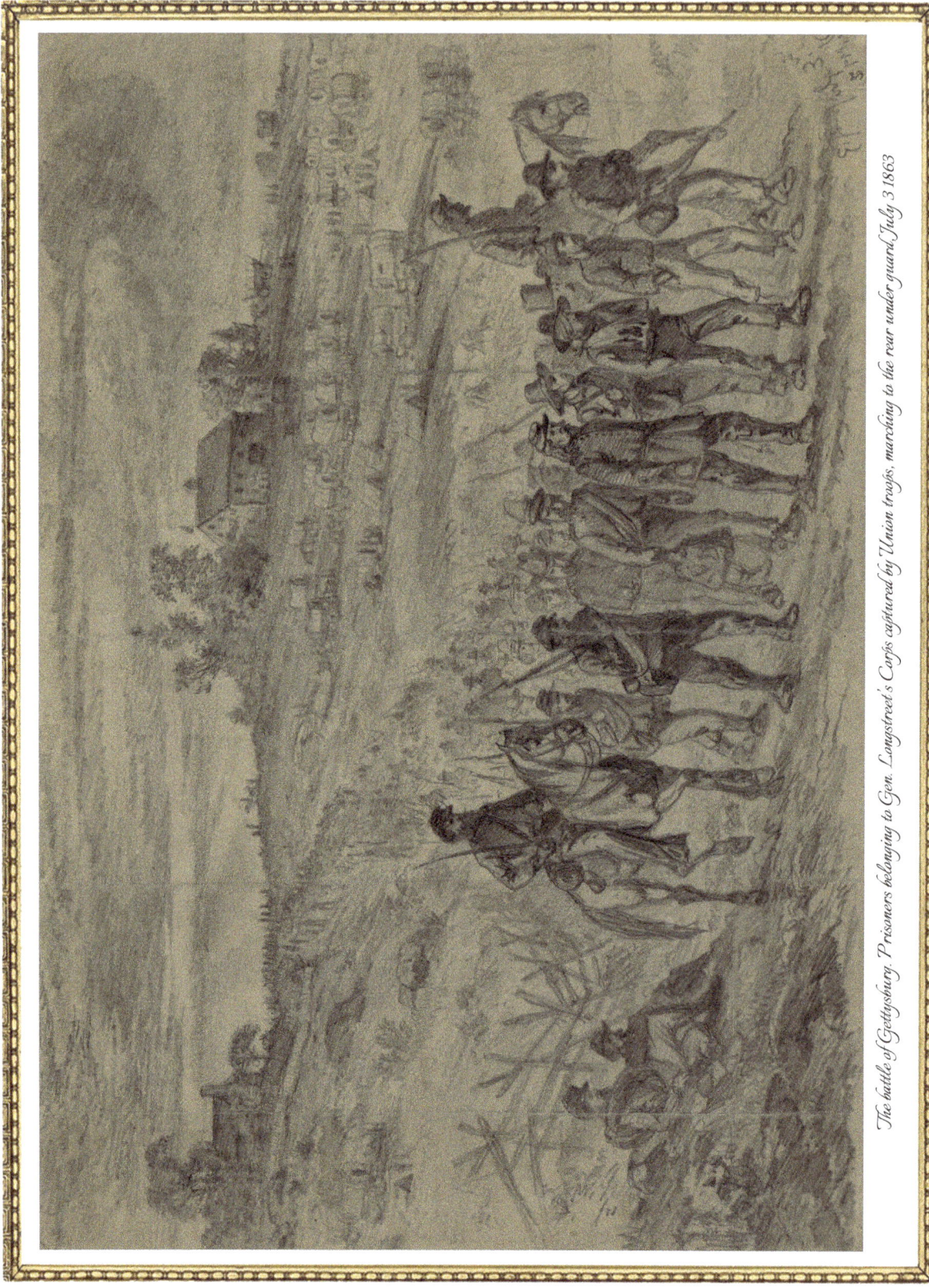

The battle of Gettysburg. Prisoners belonging to Gen. Longstreet's Corps captured by Union troops, marching to the rear under guard, July 3 1863

The battle of Gettysburg. View of Little Round Top and the Devil's Den, held by the Fifth Corps July 4 1863

Prisoners captured at Woodstock, Va., 1862

Caisson and battery horses, near the grove of trees; scene of Pickett's charge, July 4 1863

Last stand of the Army of Virginia, commanded by General Lee, July 4 1863

Escape of the Army of Virginia, commanded by General Lee, over the Potomac River near Williamsport July 4 1863

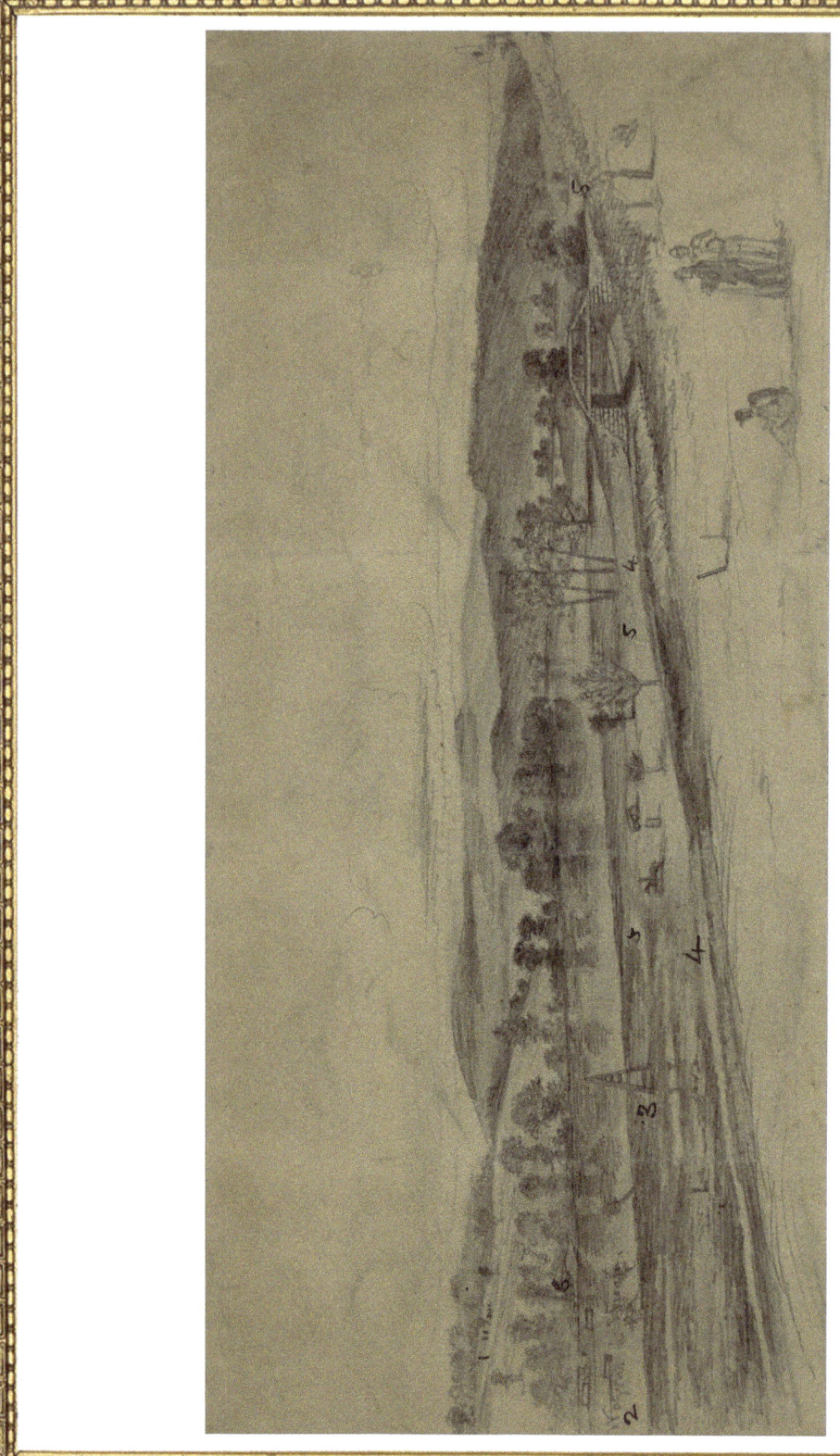

The Potomac River, near Williamsport, on the morning of the crossing of Gen. Lee's army, July 5 1863

Pursuit of Lee's army. Scene on the road near Emmitsburg, marching through the rain, July 7 1863

Sketch map of the battle of Gettysburg, made while on the march toward Frederick, Md., July 8 1863

The pursuit of Gen. Lee's rebel army. The heavy guns - 30 pounders - going to the front during a rain storm, July 10 1863

The 6th Corps (Genl. Sedgwick) crossing the bridge at Funkstown (Antietam Creek) in pursuit of Genl. Lee's forces after Gettysburg, July 12 1863

Signal officers, in attic of farm house, watching the army of General Lee near Williamsport, Maryland July 12 1863

Gallant charge by two companies of the 6th Michigan on Tuesday morning on the rebel rearguard, near Falling Waters, where part of the rebel army crossed the Potomac, July 14 1863

The First and Sixth NYV throwing pontoon bridge across the Rappahannock River near Beverly Ford, August 8 1863

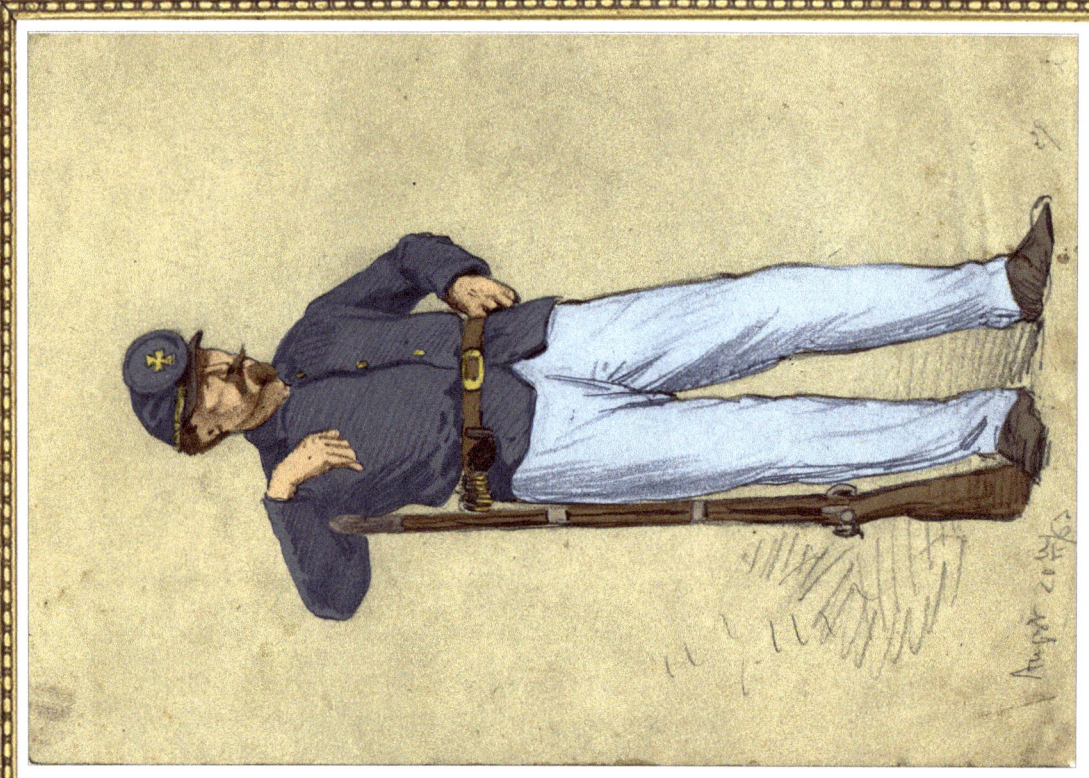

Infantryman on guard, August 1863

A Yankee volunteer, August 10 1863

Study of drummer boys on the march, August 11 1863

Sentry walking his beat, August 15 1863

The camp barber, taking a shave, Saturday, Rappahannock Station, Va., August 15 1863

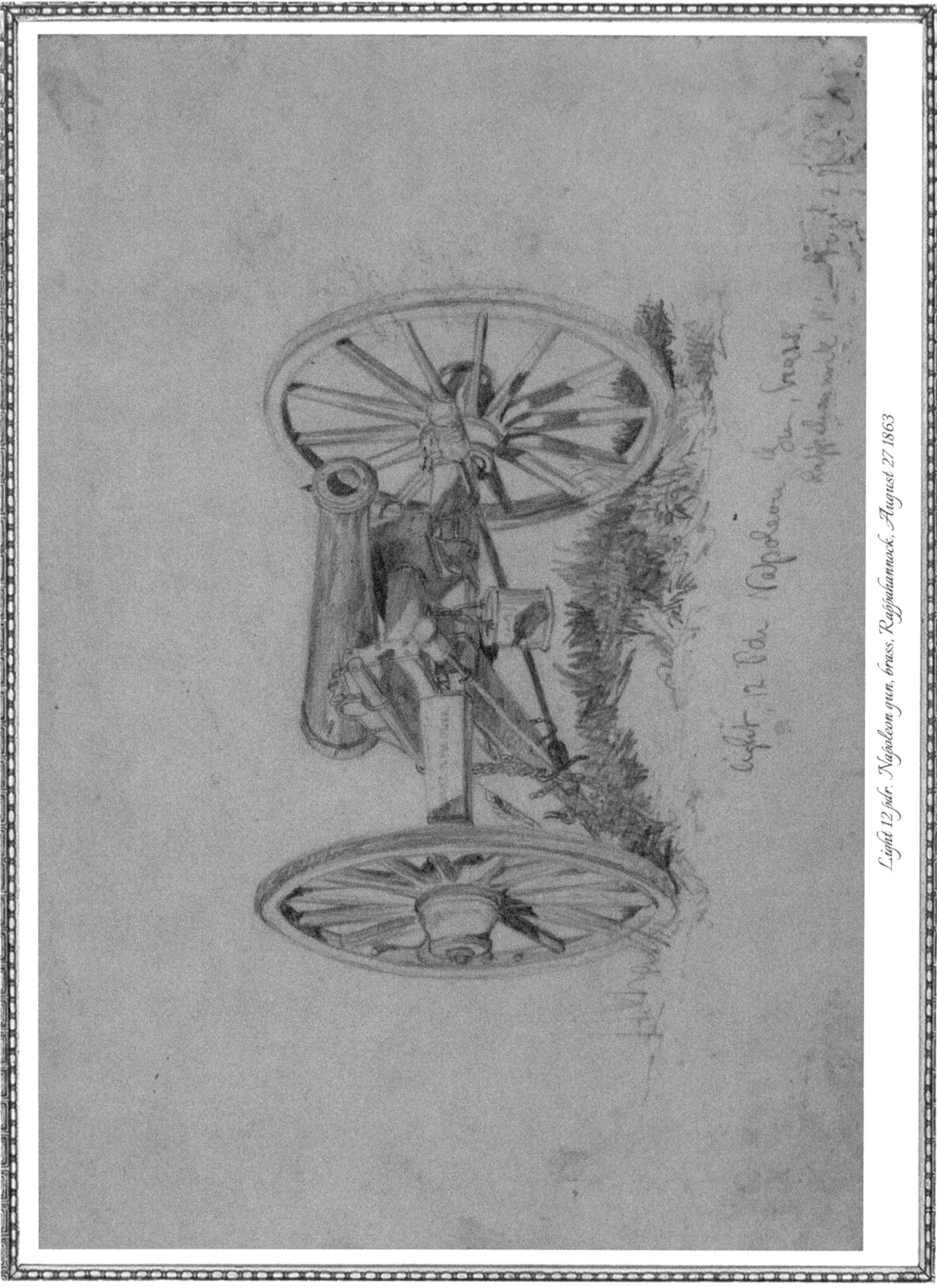

Light 12 pdr. Napoleon gun, brass, Rappahannock, August 27 1863

On guard - Aug. 27, 1863

Procession for the execution of five deserters from the 118th Pennsylvania Volunteers, 1st Division, 5th Corps, Beverly Ford, Va., August 29 1863

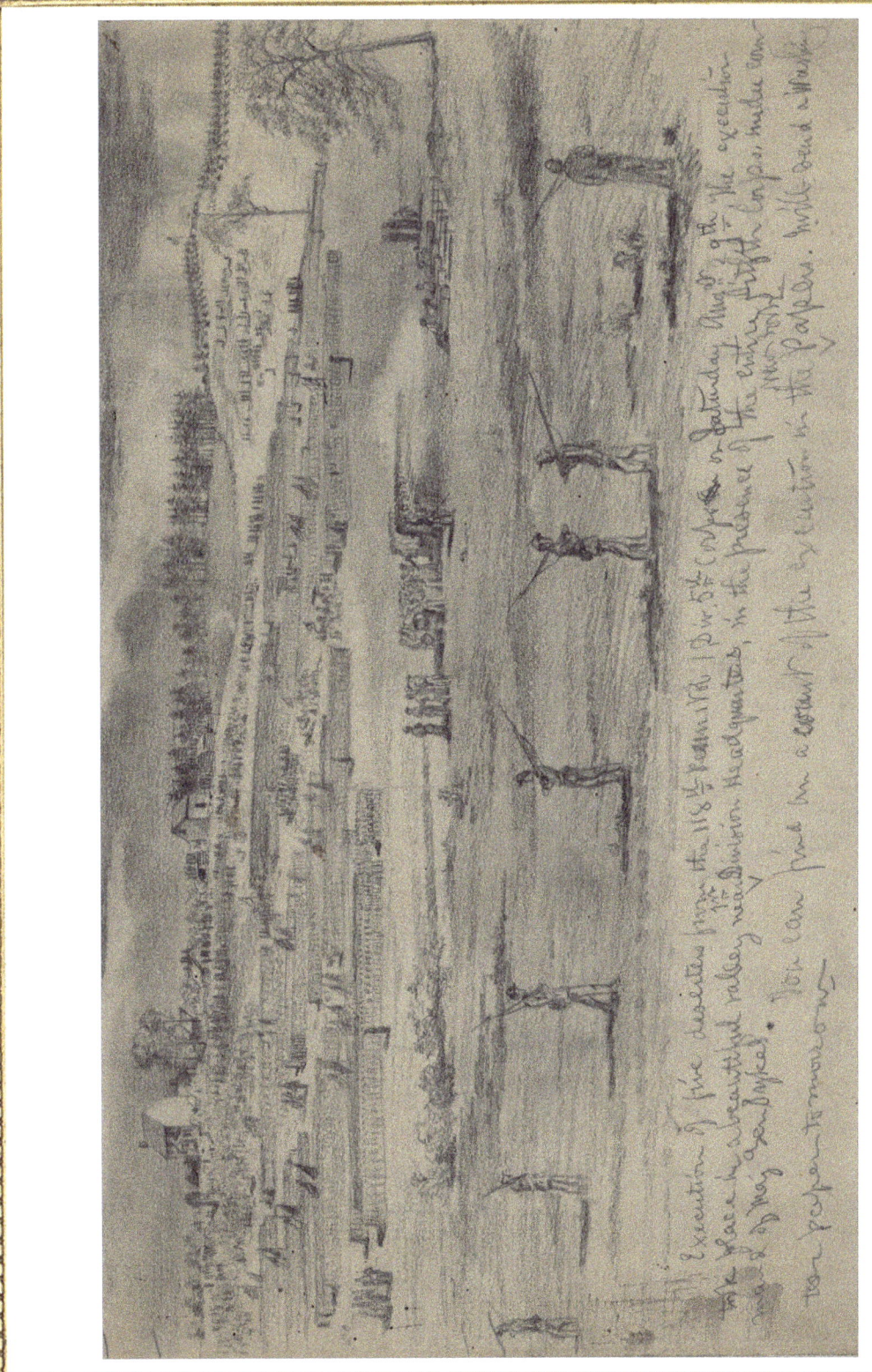

Execution of five deserters from the 118th Pennsylvania Volunteers, 1st Division, 5th Corps, before the entire 5th Corps, Beverly Ford, Va., August 29 1863

View of Centreville Va. Bull Run battlefield in the distance. Aug. 1863

Officers and soldiers on the battlefield of the second Bull Run, recognizing the remains of their comrades, August 1863 ok

Cavalry charge near Culpeper Court House, Va. September 14 1863

Brandy Station, on the Orange and Alexandria R.R. Light artillery going to the front, September 15 1863

Cavalry reconnaissance to Culpepper Court House, Va., September 16 1863

Papers in camp, Campmen, Rappahannock Station, September 18 1863

Signal station on the south side of the Rappahannock River. Seen through a glass from the Union camps, September 20 1863

Going to the commissary's, September 25 1863

Cavalry orderly waiting for orders, September 26 1863

Cavalryman escort, Culpeper, September 19 1863

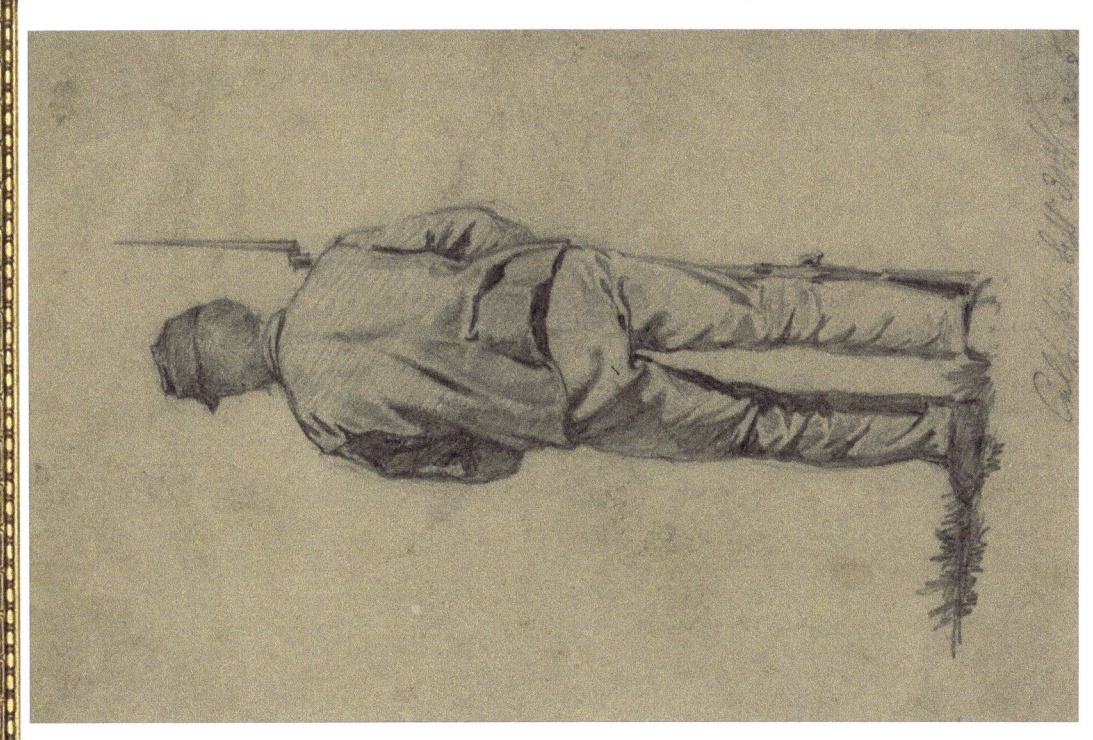

Infantryman on guard, Culpeper Court House, Va., September 30 1863

Drummer boy, Culpeper, September 29 1863

The Army of the Potomac crossing the Rappahannock River. Retreat from Culpepper to Centreville, October 13 1863

The Army of the Potomac crossing Broad Run. Retreat from Culpepper, October 14 1863

The Army of the Potomac crossing the Rappahannock River on a pontoon bridge at night, near Rappahannock Station, October 14 1863

The Army of the Potomac crossing Kettle Run, October 14 1863

The Army of the Potomac marching over the second Bull Run battleground near Groveton, October 20 1863

The battle of Rappahannock Station. Scene of Sunday in front of the works, November 8 1863

Signal officers watching the camps of Gen. Lee's army on the south side of the Rapidan River from the signal station on Poney Mountain, 11 November 1863

A cavalry vidette. Taking it easy, November 12 1863

Shoeing a mule, December 10 1863

ACW BOOKS ALREADY PUBLISHED OR IN WORKING FROM SOLDIERSHOP

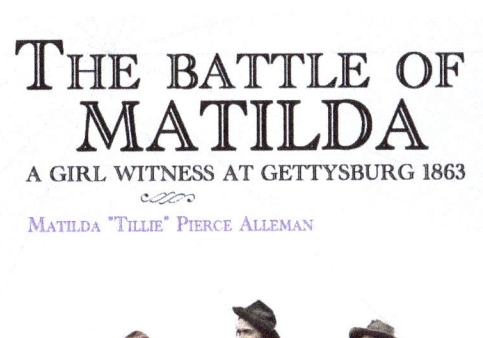

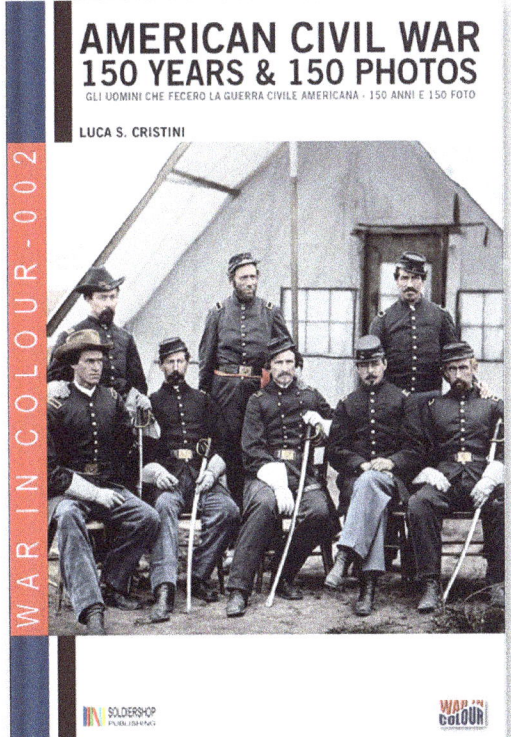
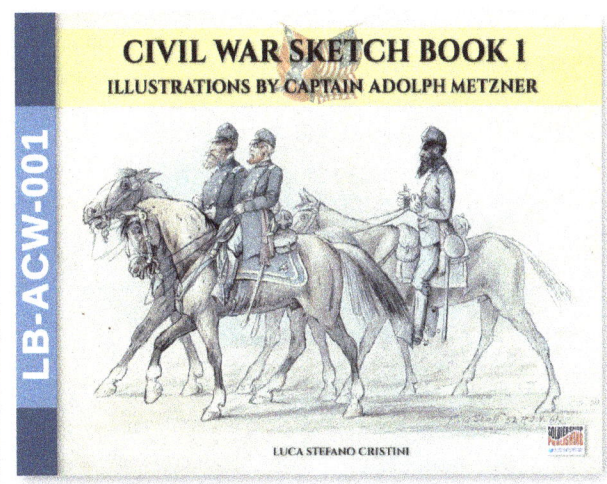
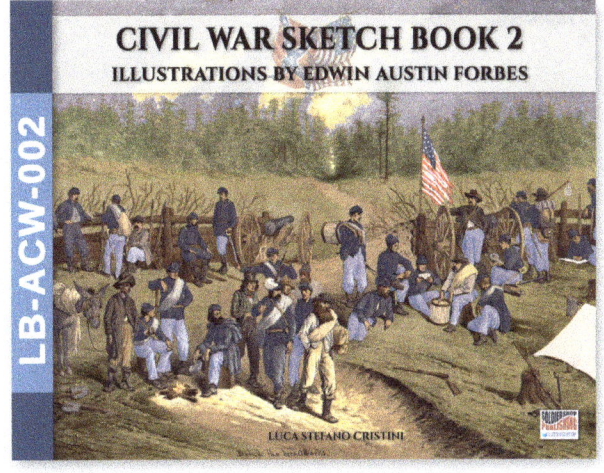

www.ingramcontent.com/pod-product-compliance
Lightning Source LLC
LaVergne TN
LVHW070527070526
838199LV00073B/6721